Decoding Daniel

Reclaiming the Visions of Daniel 7–11

Ernest Lucas

Vice-Principal, Bristol Baptist College

GROVE BOOKS LIMITED
RIDLEY HALL RD CAMBRIDGE CB3 9HU

Contents

The Cover Illustration is by Peter Ashton

First Impression December 2000
ISSN 1365-490X
ISBN 1 85174 452 5

1
Introduction

Daniel is one of the best known Old Testament books because of the stories in chapters 1–6. Their vividness, use of suspense and cartoon-like way in which the characters are portrayed make them a favourite with children. Perhaps because they have been thought of as 'children's stories,' they have not been studied much in depth until fairly recently. The rise in interest in literary approaches to the Bible has resulted in scholars beginning to appreciate the more subtle aspects of their literary artistry and dig deeper into their theological message. In principle, the issues involved in the interpretation of the stories in Daniel are the same as those for all biblical narratives, so they will not be discussed in this booklet.[1] Instead we are going to concentrate on the chapters in Daniel which present the reader with challenging problems of interpretation for which there is less help available at a fairly popular level.

The bizarre imagery, the symbolic use of numbers and the enigmatic language in the dreams and visions of chapters 7, 8, 9 and 11 have repelled some readers and attracted others. While some have neglected them, others have found them a happy hunting ground for all kinds of weird and wonderful interpretations. This has been the cause of much controversy about the book of Daniel. Behind the writing of this booklet lies the conviction that these chapters of Daniel have suffered much abuse at the hands of those who have approached it as 'decoders' rather than 'interpreters.' If approached using some of the well-tried methods of interpretation these chapters yield good sense and profound theological insights. While on the surface they may seem to offer little for the preacher, the theological insights they contain provide rich preaching material. For this reason each of the following chapters ends with some suggestions for the preacher. They could also be used as a basis for discussion in Bible study groups.

Different approaches will be used in each of the following chapters to explore the different visions. In chapter 2, an appreciation of the *cultural background* of the imagery help clarify the visions in Daniel 7 and 8. In chapter 3, consideration of the *biblical roots* of Daniel's 'seventy weeks of years' suggests a symbolic meaning for them in Daniel 9 which makes far more sense than attempts to 'decode' them as if they were some kind of cipher. In chapter 4, the *literary form* and particular literary features of the surveys of history in Daniel 8 and 11 help indicate what the author is seeking to convey.

---

1   On the interpretation of stories see Philip Jenson, *Reading Jonah* (Grove booklet B 14) chapters 3, 6.

2
Daniel 7 and 8: Culture and Communication

The vivid, and to some degree bizarre, imagery that is the most striking feature of the visions in chapters 7 and 8 has no specific background in the Hebrew Bible. The imagery could, of course, be quite unprecedented, but it is more likely that it is imagery that was familiar to the author—whether it came out of his mind as a genuine vision or (as some have argued) as a purely literary creation. And if the visions were meant to convey something to the readers of the reports of the visions, they would do that more effectively if they drew on imagery that the readers shared with the author.

Knowing the background of the imagery would help our understanding of the visions on two levels. Most obviously, if the imagery is drawn from a particular complex of ideas it would enable us to grasp the main thrust of the message. For example, as an English person newly arrived in the USA I found the appearance of donkeys and elephants in certain newspaper cartoons puzzling, until I was told that they were the traditional symbols of the two main political parties. Once I had been told that, I could grasp the political point being made by the cartoonist. Secondly, if these complexes and ideas are ones that are deeply rooted in the culture shared by the author and readers this imagery will have associated with it certain sentiments and values. This enables it to communicate at a deeper level than a superficial 'A = B,' or 'this is that,' interpretation would indicate. Goldingay expresses this aspect of the imagery well when he says, 'The symbols are not a random allegorical code speaking of realities that could just as adequately be referred to directly; they contribute to the text's meaning.'[2] The images are not like ciphers in a code whose meaning is exhausted once the code has been broken. Because of their cultural context they carry 'resonances' or have a 'feel' about them that simple ciphers do not have. This is what, in technical terms, makes some images 'symbols' rather than just 'ciphers.' As a result they have an evocative quality that communicates beyond the purely rational level to those who share their cultural context. Of course, just because they are culturally conditioned, it is these non-cipher, symbolic, aspects of the imagery that are hard for us to discern. As a result, we may go for a simple 'decoding' approach. The problem is then compounded since we will probably be guided in this by *our* cultural conditioning when choosing the 'key' to 'crack the code.' My natural assumption that 'donkey = stupid' and 'elephant = good memory' did not provide the right 'keys' to understand the cartoon imagery

2   J E Goldingay, *Daniel* (Dallas: Word Books, 1989) p 148.

in the USA!

The search to capture something of the wider, culturally embedded, symbolic significance of the imagery in these visions has led to an extensive debate about their religio-historical background. One might question the value of all this discussion and debate. After all, the symbols are interpreted within the visions. But this interpretation only settles the question of the *reference* (the 'this is that' aspect) of the symbolic imagery. If what has been said in the previous paragraph is valid, it still leaves open the possibility that the imagery carried a wider meaning that would be sensed by the author and original readers because of the significance of these images as symbols in their culture. This is a possibility that is at least worth exploring.

Daniel 7.1–8: The Animal Imagery

There is not space here to discuss all the possible sources of the imagery that have been proposed and debated. I have done that at length elsewhere.[3] Here I will simply summarize the conclusions reached in that discussion.

For over a century a number of scholars have seen the Babylonian creation story *Enuma Elish* as the source of the imagery in chapter 7 of hybrid beasts rising out of a turbulent sea. In this story Marduk, the patron god of Babylon, defeats the forces of chaos, which are depicted as a horde of hybrid creatures within the primeval waters. They are led by the primeval goddess Tiamat. Marduk slays Tiamat, with the aid of the four winds of heaven, and splits her body in two. With one half he makes the earth and with the other the dome of the sky. He then proceeds with other acts of creation, including the creation of humans as the virtual slaves of the gods. They are created to provide the gods with houses (temples), and keep them supplied with food and drink (offerings). This creation story probably existed in variant forms throughout the ancient Near-East. Imagery reminiscent of it occurs in Hebrew poetry which speaks of Yahweh as Creator (Job 26.12–13; Psalms 74.12–14; 89.9–11; Isaiah 51.9). Although this imagery was very probably known and used by the Hebrews before the Babylonian exile[4] it would be particularly relevant and evocative for the Jews living as exiles in Babylon.[5] A high point of the Babylonian year was a great New Year Festival which was celebrated in Babylon and of which *Enuma Elish* was the liturgy. The story was

---

3   E C Lucas, 'The Source of Daniel's Animal Imagery,' *Tyndale Bulletin* 41 (1990) pp 161–185.
4   They may have adopted and adapted it from its use in Canaanite culture. The Ugaritic texts contain a story of a conflict between Baal and the Sea and also allusions to a defeat of Leviathan by Baal. These have similarities to *Enuma Elish* but do not, in their extant form, include an account of creation. See J Day, *God's Conflict with the Dragon and the Sea* (Cambridge: CUP, 1985) especially chapter 1.
5   The possibility of direct Babylonian influence on Daniel 7.2ff is suggested by the phrase 'the four winds of heaven.' This is quite a common phrase in Babylonian literature, but is not found in Ugaritic literature. Outside Daniel it occurs in Hebrew only in Zechariah 2.6 (MT 2.10), which has a Babylonian background.

probably acted out in some way. Therefore the imagery of the first part of the vision in chapter 7 would be evocative of the themes of chaos and creation, and of the question of which god is able to transform chaos into cosmos—ordered creation.

Bizarre hybrid creatures are a feature of Mesopotamian art and literature. A likely reason for this is the important role that 'birth omens' played in Mesopotamian divination.[6] Omen priests who specialized in this form of divination examined any malformed new born creatures, whether live or still-born, to discern their ominous meaning. It was probably in the aborted foetuses of domestic animals that they saw various animal forms that do have some resemblance to Daniel's beasts. None of the hybrid creatures described in extant omens exactly matches any of those in Daniel. But in a culture used to birth omens, 'the animal anomalies in [Daniel's] visions originally had an evocative power by virtue of their stylistic dependence on Mesopotamian omen literature, rather than because of any perceived literal absurdity.'[7] While the animal imagery in Daniel might catch our attention simply because it is bizarre, for readers used to Babylonian omens it would evoke a sense of the numinous and ominous, and so compel attention. This would probably be as true for Jews who had lived in exile in Babylon for any length of time as for the local population.[8]

Neither of these Babylonian backgrounds throws light on the number, sequence and basic character of the beasts in Daniel 7.2ff. Here some scholars have seen the influence of Hosea 13.7–8, where Yahweh declares, 'So I will become like a lion to them, like a leopard I will lurk beside the way. I will fall on them like a bear robbed of her cubs, and will tear open the covering of their heart; there I will devour them like a lion, as a wild animal would mangle them.' In this verse we have the four beasts of Daniel chapter 7: lion, leopard, bear and an unnamed wild beast. The change of order in Daniel may be because elsewhere in the Hebrew Bible the lion and bear are usually mentioned together as the two most ferocious beasts. All this suggests that in some way Yahweh is at work in the wild beasts of Daniel's imagery even though they appear to be opposed to his people and purposes.

Although an astrological basis has been suggested for the use of the ram and goat in chapter 8, the evidence for this is not very convincing.[9] It more likely arises from the use of these animals as symbols of power, and so occa-

6 E Leichty, *The Omen Series Shumma Izbu* (Locust Valley, NY: J J Augustin, 1970) p 14, comments that, 'Outside Mesopotamia birth omens seem to have been unimportant except to the Hittites and later Etruscans and Romans.'

7 P A Porter, *Metaphors and Monsters* (Toronto: Porter, 1985) p 29.

8 I am assuming that Daniel's visions originated with a Jew living in Babylon, whether they date to the sixth or the second century BCE. I have argued the case for this in: E C Lucas, 'Daniel: Resolving the Enigma,' *Vetus Testamentum* 50 (2000) pp 66–80.

9 See Lucas, 'The Source of Daniel's Animal Imagery,' pp 177–182.

sionally of leadership (Ezekiel 34.17; 39.18; Zechariah 10.3). There is more of the 'cipher' quality to the imagery in this chapter because what is said of the horns of each animal clearly relates to historical actualities, as vv 20–22 make clear. But identifying the horns with particular kings and kingdoms does not exhaust the meaning of the imagery, because in the ancient Near-East the horn was a potent symbol of strength and power.

Daniel 7.9–14: The Throne Scene

There has been extensive debate about the possible background of the imagery of the throne scene in Daniel 7.9–14, and I will not attempt to survey it here.[10] There is a general agreement that some of the imagery has a background in Canaanite culture. The stock epithet for Baal in the Ugaritic texts is 'rider/charioteer of the clouds.' Epithets for the chief of the pantheon, El, include 'judge,' 'father,' and 'father of years,' and he is portrayed as an aged (and therefore wise) person. If this view is valid, it suggests that the imagery about the 'Ancient of Days' and the one 'coming with the clouds of heaven' would have strong numinous associations.

There are similarities between Daniel's vision of the thrones and Ezekiel's vision of Yahweh's chariot throne. In Ezekiel 1 there is a stormy wind, four animal-like creatures, each with four different faces and wings. In the middle of them there are burning coals of fire. Above them there is a throne with more fire and a human-like figure. In Ezekiel the prophet is often addressed by God as *ben 'adham* ('son of man'), the Hebrew equivalent of the Aramaic phrase *bar 'enosh* used in Daniel 7.13. Its use in Ezekiel seems to emphasize the prophet's humanness, and perhaps weakness, over against the deity. The weakness and general unimpressiveness of humans is expressed by the same phrase in Psalm 8.5 (where the phrase is used in parallel with *'enosh*). In this psalm there are strong associations with Genesis 1.26–28, which speaks of God's purposes for human beings as viceroys over the created order. The phrase *ben 'adham* also occurs in Psalm 80.17 (MT 80.18), where it refers to either Israel or the king, 'Let your hand be on the man of your right hand, upon the son of man you have made strong for yourself' (my translation). In either case, the context makes 'the son of man' a figure standing for the suffering people of Yahweh, who are pleading for deliverance from oppression.

In Daniel 7.13 the phrase *bar 'enosh* emphasizes the human-like nature of the figure who receives the ultimate kingdom over against the bestial nature of the historical kingdoms. The use of this phrase, which evokes Psalm 8, and through it Genesis 1.26–28, indicates that this is a vision about the consummation of Yahweh's purpose in creating the world. At the same time it is a vision about Yahweh saving his people from oppression. This is explicit in

---

10   There is a useful survey in J J Collins, *Daniel* (Minneapolis: Fortress Press, 1993) pp 280–294.

the interpretation in vv 21, 25–27. This vision, therefore, brings together the two great biblical themes of creation and salvation. Through his saving acts Yahweh brings to completion the purpose he had when he created the world.

Daniel 7 and the Preacher

Daniel 7 provides the preacher with a general lesson—the importance of imagery in communication. Well-chosen symbolic imagery communicates far more than can be spelled out in prosaic words, and does so powerfully if the imagery is deeply rooted in the culture shared by speaker and hearers. This challenges us to consider what images there are in our culture that we can use in our teaching and preaching in order to increase the power and depth of our communication.

Congregations can be helped to appreciate the 'symbolic' rather than 'cipher' quality of the imagery in Daniel by careful use of examples of symbolic images used in modern forms of communication. Two fruitful sources of examples are newspaper cartoons, especially the more political ones,[11] and advertisements. Both of these forms of communication tend to make use of stereotypical images that evoke more general images that have deep cultural roots.

There are several rich theological themes in this passage, which the preacher can develop.

- Humans were created in the image of God to have dominion over creation as God's representatives. However, when they exercise that dominion without reference to God and for their own ends they tend to become sub-human, bestial, in their behaviour. (This is underlined by the allusion in the imagery about the first beast to Nebuchadnezzar's experience recorded in chapter 4). Instead of promoting the harmony of creation they become agents of chaos.
- The imagery of Daniel 7.1–8 invites us to examine the difficulty we have in holding on to the transcendent dimension of reality in which 'God is still on the throne' when the political beasts seem to be rampaging about unchecked. How can we deal with this?
- Even more challenging is the implication of Hosea 13.7–8 that, while being agents of chaos, the beasts may also be the agents of the Creator! God certainly used Nebuchadnezzar of Babylon and Cyrus of Persia to forward his purposes.
- The integral relationship between God's purposes in creation and salvation has particular relevance in the light of the ecological crises which

---

11 For discussion of this see: D S Russell, 'Apocalyptic Imagery as Political Cartoon?' in J Barton and D J Reimer (eds), *After the Exile* (Macon, Ga: Mercer University Press, 1996) pp 191–200.

threaten the world today. Salvation embraces the renewal of the whole of creation, not just the saving of individual human beings. Therefore to work for that renewal now is to provide a sign of the kingdom of God, in the same way that working for justice in human society provides such a sign.

- This is not a triumphalist text, though it may seem so on the surface. Although God's ultimate purpose triumphs and his people are given 'dominion and glory and kingship' and 'an everlasting kingdom' it is made clear in vv 21, 25–27 that suffering precedes glory. The link with Psalm 80.17 supports this.

Postscript: The Four Kingdoms

So far nothing has been said about the identification of the four kingdoms represented by the beasts. This has been deliberate, to show that the main theological thrust of the vision does not depend on resolving this 'decoding' issue, on which much ink has been spilt. However, perhaps it should not be ignored altogether.

The major commentaries can be consulted for the detailed arguments. The echoes of Daniel 4 in what is said of the first beast make it clear that the beast represents the Babylonian Empire. The two beasts in chapter 8 are identified as the Medo-Persian and Greek Empires. There is little doubt that the 'small horn' in chapter 8 is Antiochus Epiphanes. He ruled one of the kingdoms that arose out of the break-up of Alexander the Great's empire, and instigated a severe persecution of the Jews in 167–164 BCE. There are many correspondences between this 'little horn' and the 'little horn' that arises from the fourth beast in chapter 7. There are also some differences, but they can be seen as references to complementary aspects of Antiochus' personality and career, not as contradictions. This points to the fourth beast being representative of the Greek Empire, which fits with it being 'different from all the beasts that preceded it' (7.7), since it was a European power, not a Near-Eastern one.

This makes the sequence of the empires represented by the beasts: Babylonian, Median, Persian, Greek. It is sometimes objected that there was no Median Empire between the Babylonian and the Persian. That reflects a very tidy, linear view of history. The reality was that the Babylonian and Median Empires came into being more or less at the same time; they combined to overthrow Assyria and carved up the Assyrian Empire between them. Babylonian power declined markedly after Nebuchadnezzar's death while both the power and extent of the Median Empire continued to grow. Media was the effective superpower in the Near-East from the time of Nebuchadnezzar's death until Cyrus, a Median vassal, and half-Median himself, rebelled and took over the Empire. His Medo-Persian Empire continued on the trajectory set in place by his predecessors and eventually swallowed up the much weakened Babylonian Empire.

In 2 Esdras (= 4 Ezra) 12.11–12 the author makes clear that in identifying Daniel's fourth beast with the Roman Empire he is doing something new. It had not been understood in that way before. It is understandable that Jews and Christians found it possible to re-apply the imagery of the fourth beast to later powers that emulated Antiochus' arrogance and godlessness, starting with Roman actions against the Jews (2 Esdras/4 Ezra 12) and Christians (Revelation 13). Nor is it surprising that the 'little horn' becomes the archetype of the anti-Christ. These are legitimate *re-applications* of the imagery which accord with the theological thrust of the vision. But I would want to distinguish them from the *original* meaning of the vision itself (in terms of the referents of the symbols), and not claim that one of them is the 'real' interpretation of it to the exclusion of any other.

3
Daniel 9: Scripture Re-applied

The re-application of imagery mentioned at the end of the last chapter is something which happens within the Bible itself. An example of this is Jeremiah's prophecy that the Babylonian exile would last seventy years. If we follow the indications of date in the text of Jeremiah as it stands, he twice spoke of the exile lasting seventy years, in 605 BCE (Jeremiah 25.11) and again in 594 BCE (29.10). There is general agreement among the commentators that the figure was intended as a round one, indicating 'a lifetime.' This certainly makes sense in the context of the 'Letter to the Exiles' in Jeremiah 29. Here the prophet's main concern is to combat false prophecies of a speedy return to Judah. He does this by telling them to settle down and build homes and establish a way of life in Babylon because they are going to be there a long time. This 'round number' reading of the figure also fits with Jeremiah's statement that the Babylonian Empire would last for three generations (Jeremiah 27.7). If one dates the exile from the first deportation (596/7) to the first return (538) it actually lasted about 59 years.

A different, and deeply symbolic, understanding of the seventy years is expressed in 2 Chronicles 36.19–23. In this text the period from the destruction of the Jerusalem and the Temple (586/7) to the first return (538) is related to the land needing to make up its lost Sabbaths. The fact that this is said to be fulfilled by the seventy years prophesied by Jeremiah implies that the number is understood symbolically as ten sabbatical cycles, a 'complete' period of rest for the land.

Yet another understanding of the seventy years is found in Zech 1.12. This is a plea to Yahweh to end his anger with 'the cities of Judah' and the mention of seventy years is clearly an allusion to Jeremiah's prophecy. This plea is part of a vision dated to 520 BCE, and so close to seventy years after the destruction of Jerusalem and the Temple. In the context of Zechariah 1–8, the seventy years seems to be understood as the actual period between the destruction of the Temple (586/7) and the completion of its rebuilding (516).

Daniel's 'Seventy Sevens'

Daniel 9 contains a great prayer of confession and supplication which is prompted by Jeremiah's prophecy of seventy years of devastation for Jerusalem. In response to this prayer Daniel receives a visit from the angel Gabriel who conveys to him an enigmatic message about 'seventy sevens' that are 'decreed for your people and your holy city' (9.24–27). The word 'sevens' can mean 'weeks' (as it does in Daniel 10.2), and there is general agreement that the phrase 'seventy sevens/weeks' means 'seventy weeks of years' by analogy with the 'seventy weeks of years' in Leviticus 25.8.

Down the centuries these few verses of Daniel have spawned a vast amount of literature and debate. Sadly, it has often been polemical and divisive. They were used as part of the anti-establishment polemic of Fifth Monarchists and other Separatists in the 17th century. Sir Isaac Newton was only one of many Protestant scholars who made them part of a strong anti-Catholic polemic in the 17th and 18th centuries.[12] In the 19th and 20th centuries they featured in the 'dispensationalist' debates that sometimes caused deep divisions in the Evangelical wing of the church, especially in the Free Churches. Any preacher or Bible study leader who deals with these verses needs to be aware of the main lines of the more recent different interpretations that might be in the minds of those in the congregation or Bible study group.

Most scholars have assumed that Daniel 9.24–27 is intended as a strict chronology of events and there have been numerous different attempts to interpret it in this vein.[13] All of them face a major problem in deciding the point at which to begin their chronology—'the time that the word went out to restore and build Jerusalem' (Daniel 9.25). The possibilities that have been employed are (with dates given first):

605	Jeremiah's prophecy in Jeremiah 25.12.
597	The first deportation, referred to in Jeremiah 29.10.
594?	The sending of Jeremiah's 'Letter to the Exiles.'
586/7	Jeremiah's prophecies of restoration in Jeremiah 30.18–22; 31.38–40.
539?	Gabriel's own words to Daniel.
539	Cyrus' decree recorded in Ezra 1.1–4.
521	Darius' decree recorded in Ezra 6.1–12.
458	Artaxerxes' decree recorded in Ezra 7.12–26.
445	Artaxerxes' warrant given to Nehemiah in Nehemiah 2.7–8.

One issue in the debate is whether the use of the term 'word' in Daniel 9.25, rather than one of the more specific terms for a royal decree, means that a prophetic 'word of Yahweh' is what is meant. Another is the fact that only Jeremiah's prophecies of restoration and Artaxerxes' warrant of 445 actually mention the rebuilding of Jerusalem.

There have been two main lines of chronological interpretation of the 'seventy weeks of years,' which I have labelled 'messianic' and 'Maccabean' respectively. Within each there are a number of variant versions.

---

12 S J Barnett (ed), *Isaac Newton's Observations on the Prophecies of Daniel and the Apocalypse of St John* (Lampeter: Edwin Mellen Press, 1999).

13 J A Montgomery, *The Book of Daniel* (Edinburgh: T and T Clark, 1964) pp 390–401 surveys interpretations up to 1926. This can be supplemented by the discussions in: E J Young, *Daniel* (Edinburgh: Banner of Truth, 1988) pp 191–195; J G Baldwin, *Daniel* (Leicester: IVP, 1978) pp 172–178; A Y Collins in the reference in footnote 12, pp 112–123.

The Messianic Interpretation

The 'messianic' interpretation appears in Christian exegesis towards the end of the second century. One factor that encouraged it was the translation of 9.25 in the dominant Greek translation of Daniel (Theodotion's). This takes the 'seven weeks and sixty-two weeks' as a unit: '…until Christ the chief, seven weeks and sixty-two weeks.' This prompted Christian exegetes to see the coming of Jesus as end-point of this period of 69 'weeks of years.' The problem was fixing the starting point. In modern times this has been taken to be either Artaxerxes' commission to Ezra in 458 or his warrant to Nehemiah in 445. The former date has the disadvantage that the commission does not mention rebuilding Jerusalem, but the advantage that 483 years (69x7) later (remembering that there was no 'year 0' at the turn of the eras) comes to 26 CE, a possible date for the beginning of Jesus' public ministry. His death in 30 CE (a possible, though disputed, date) is then taken to occur in the middle of the final week, the other half of the week being postponed into the indefinite future. Starting with 445, when permission was given to rebuild Jerusalem, faces the problem that 483 years later comes to 39 CE. This problem is 'solved' by postulating that the years of the prophecy are 'prophetic years' of 360 days only, so bringing the date down to 32 CE. This is taken as the date of Jesus' death, with the whole of the final week postponed to the indefinite future. The appeal to these 'prophetic years' rests on the fact that, at various times and places in the ancient Near-East, calendars with twelve months of thirty days were used. However, it was always recognized that these 'civil' calendars ran out of step with the 'real world' and various schemes of inter-calary days or months were used to correct for this. It is very unlikely that anyone would use a 360-day year in chronological calculations.

Furthermore, the 'messianic' approach faces problems other than those of chronology.

- There seems to be no point in saying 'seven weeks and sixty-two weeks' unless something is going to happen after the seven. The NRSV translation ('until the time of an anointed prince, there shall be seven weeks; and for sixty-two weeks it shall be built again with streets and moat, but in a troubled time') is therefore more natural than that of the NIV ('until the Anointed One, the ruler, comes, there will be seven "sevens" and sixty-two "sevens." It will be rebuilt with streets and a trench, but in times of trouble').[14]

---

14 Despite what E J Young says (*Daniel*, p 205), taking 'and sixty-two weeks' as an accusative of time ('then for sixty-two weeks') is in accord with the rules of Hebrew syntax. Many early Christian exegetes who knew Theodotion's Greek translation still took the verse to imply two separate periods, not one unbroken period.

- In context, the most likely referent for 'the word' in v 25 is the prophecies of Jeremiah. It is pondering 'the word of Yahweh to Jeremiah' that leads to Daniel's prayer and the revelation through Gabriel.
- The need to introduce an indefinite 'time chasm' either before or in the middle of the final week when nothing like this is implied in the text.
- The absence of any clear interest in a truly 'messianic' figure elsewhere in Daniel.

The Maccabean Interpretation

The 'Maccabean' interpretation takes the last week of the seventy to include the period of the persecution of the Jews by Antiochus Epiphanes in 167–164 BCE. It is implied by 1 Maccabees 1.54, with its allusion to the 'desolating sacrilege' of Daniel 9.27. Porphyry, a pagan opponent of Christianity, argued for it in the late third century CE, as did the Christian scholar Julius Hilarianus in the late fourth century. However, no doubt partly in reaction to Porphyry, it was largely ignored until modern times. Modern versions of this approach take 'the word' of v 25 to be one of Jeremiah's prophecies. The 'anointed one' who comes at the end of the first seven weeks is identified with one of the major figures involved in the initial return from exile: Cyrus (called 'his [ie Yahweh's] anointed' in Isaiah 45.1), Zerubbabel or Joshua (Joshua was the High Priest and both are called 'sons of oil' in Zechariah 4.14). Defined in this way the exile did last about 49 (7x7) years (586/7–539/8). The 'anointed one' who is 'cut off' after the subsequent sixty-two weeks is taken to be the High Priest Onias III, who was assassinated in 171. The middle of the final week then falls in 167, the year Antiochus proscribed the Jewish religion and desecrated the Temple. It ends in 164, when Judas Maccabeus rededicated the Temple and Antiochus died unexpectedly. The strength of this approach is that it avoids the exegetical objections against the 'messianic' approach and provides plausible referents for many of the allusions in the prophecy.

The major problem with the 'Maccabean' approach is that the period between the return from exile and the murder of Onias III is only 367 years, not 434 (62x7) years. This is usually explained as the result of the prophecy being a 'prophecy after the event' and the author having only a vague knowledge of the chronology of the Persian period. However, Laato has shown that Jewish writers may not have been as ignorant or mistaken about the chronology of the period as is often claimed.[15]

---

15   A Laato, 'The Seventy Yearweeks in the Book of Daniel' *Zeitschrift für die alttestamentliche Wissenschaft* 102 (1990) pp 212–225.

A Symbolic Interpretation: Chronography not Chronology

A few modern commentators of both approaches have argued that the numbers and periods should not be taken chronologically but symbolically.[16] As we have seen, Jeremiah's prophecy of seventy years of exile is understood symbolically elsewhere in the Hebrew Bible. The possible allusion to Leviticus 25.8 noted above points to a likely symbolic understanding in terms of sabbatical periods. This is strengthened by the existence of a number of verbal and thematic links between Daniel's prayer and Leviticus 26.27–45, a passage that warns of a period of divine wrath measured in sabbatical cycles.[17] In this passage the people are warned that their *covenant disloyalty* will result in *desolation*, but that if they *confess* their sins Yahweh will remember the covenant and the Promised Land. Daniel follows this pattern. He admits Israel's *covenant disloyalty*, which has brought about *desolation*, and *confesses* the nation's sin, appealing for Yahweh's mercy.

We must also take note of the fact that in the Hebrew Bible the number seven is associated with completeness, totality and perfection. This is even more so with regard to the number seventy. So, a span of seventy weeks of years represents a complete period, the one needed to bring in the perfect kingdom (Daniel 9.24). But this period (490 years) is ten jubilee cycles. The concept of jubilee is the main theme of Leviticus 25, the passage from which the concept of 'weeks of years' is taken. The jubilee year was the great year of release from debt and slavery, and restoration of family lands. So, ten jubilee cycles is an appropriate period to symbolize the coming of the ultimate act of divine deliverance and restoration. The first seven weeks (49 years) may correspond quite well to one way of measuring the exile chronologically, but the figure is probably used because it represents the 49 years that lead up to a year of jubilee, a year of release for slaves and captives. The antithesis of perfection is sometimes represented by one less than the perfect number (for example, 666 as the number of the beast in Revelation 13.18). Therefore it is appropriate that the climax of devastation comes at the end of the sixty-ninth week. The period of sixty-two weeks is simply the inevitable result of subtracting the first symbolic period (seven weeks) from the second (sixty-nine weeks). One week (seven years) provides a suitable symbolic period for sin to reach its climax and be brought to a total end. Again, it just happens that the murder of Onias III and the rededication of the Temple are separated by about seven years, with the desecration of the Temple coming, very roughly, mid-way between them.

If this symbolic understanding of Daniel 9.24–27 is correct, what we have

---

16 For example: J G Baldwin, *Daniel* (Leicester: IVP, 1978) p 176; J E Goldingay, *Daniel* (Dallas: Word Books, 1989) pp 257f.
17 M Fishbane, *Biblical Interpretation in Ancient Israel* (Oxford: Clarendon Press, 1988) pp 488f, discusses these.

in these verses is a re-application of Jeremiah's prophecy of seventy years of exile in the light of Leviticus 25 and 26 to provide an understanding of the Maccabean crisis. These verses are not intended to be a chronology of events, but a 'chronography,'[18] a symbolic scheme of history which is intended to interpret the major events in it, not provide a means of calculating when they did, or will, happen.

Scripture Re-applied Again

Daniel 9.26–27 is sufficiently allusive in its language for it to be possible to re-apply these verses to later situations where the same pattern of suffering, oppression and deliverance occurs, or is expected. As Heaton comments, the validity of such re-application is not to be decided by the 'fit' of details with Scripture so much as by the quality of the moral and spiritual judgment that is displayed.[19] It is notable that when Mark 13.14 (Matt 24.15) use the motif of 'the abomination that desolates' there is no reference to the seventy weeks of Daniel 9. It is the recurrence of the pattern of an oppression of God's people, focused on the Temple, which is being highlighted. In the gospels the hope of deliverance is rooted in what Christians see as the supreme evidence that God acts to deliver his people: the life, death and resurrection of Jesus Christ.

Daniel 9 and the Preacher

Understanding Daniel 9.24–27 as chronography rather than chronology opens up ways to preach on it. This is because it shifts the focus from a sequence of events in history to the meaning of history. The 'Jubilee 2000' campaign has made people aware of the biblical concept of jubilee as a time of release and restoration, and this can provide a way in to help people understand the interpretation of these verses in the light of the ideas of sabbatical cycles and jubilee cycles. The theological heart of the issue is what is implied here about the nature of Yahweh as a God who is characterized by acts of release and restoration. Because this is so, such acts should be part of the fabric of the society of God's people. We need to ponder how that can be realized in church life as well as (quite rightly) campaigning for it in international relations.

This chapter has concentrated on the final verses of Daniel 9, because they are so controversial. But the earlier verses are taken up with a profoundly theological prayer. There is not space to discuss its contents. We can only note that the whole chapter does raise issues about prayer that the preacher can ponder and develop.

18　See L L Grabbe, 'Chronography in Hellenistic Jewish Historiography' *Society of Biblical Literature Seminar Papers* 17 (1979) pp 43–68.
19　E W Heaton, *Daniel* (London: SCM, 1972) p 202f.

- It is significant that when Daniel reads the prophecy in Jeremiah with its promise of deliverance from exile after seventy years he does not simply 'name it and claim it.' He launches into a prayer of repentance. There is a reminder here that the Bible is not a 'promise box' full of goodies that can be 'claimed' at random and in isolation. The promises of God must be understood within the context of a biblical theology. Daniel clearly understands this promise in the context of the theology of sin-oppression-repentance-deliverance that is expressed in Leviticus 26. He realizes that the promise of deliverance cannot be abstracted and claimed apart from the recognition of sin and repentance for it.

- Some commentators take the fact that Gabriel says, 'At the *beginning* of your supplication a word went out' (v 23) to indicate that Daniel's prayer was superfluous, and that this is part of the deterministic view of history expressed in the book of Daniel. This reading is too rationalistic. It ignores the statement that follows that the 'word' has gone out because Daniel is 'greatly loved' by God. A Jew who could recite Psalm 139.4 'Even before a word is on my tongue, O Lord, you know it completely' would have no difficulty with the idea that Yahweh does not have to sit back, let Daniel finish his prayer, think about it and then respond. The Hebrews were aware that time is not the same for God as for humans (Ps. 90.4). So God's swift response to Daniel is not evidence that his prayer is ignored, but that God is eager to listen and respond. This is because of his love for Daniel. Isaiah 65.24 comes to mind, 'Before they call I will answer, while they are yet speaking I will hear.'

- This is not to deny that there is a somewhat deterministic view of history in vv 24–27. Indeed, the chronological reading of these verses can lead to a 'clockwork' view of history as following a fixed and unchangeable schema. It is a commonplace of Hebrew thought that God has a plan for history, and that Israel has a central place in it. It was also understood that God's plans cannot be thwarted, 'As I have designed so shall it be; and as I have planned so shall it come to pass…For the Lord of hosts has planned, and who will annul it?' (Isaiah 14.24–27). Yet there are times when the Hebrew prophets announce Yahweh's plan in an apparently cut-and-dried way with no room for doubt that it is going to happen, and then the human response results in a change of plan (*eg* 2 Kings 20.1–7; Jonah 3.1–10). The Hebrews were not embarrassed to speak of Yahweh 'repenting' and changing his mind (Jer 18). This, of course, causes problems if we want to have a neatly packaged theology with no loose ends. But it reflects the tension between God's sovereignty and human responsibility with which most believers are prepared to live in reality, and which is at the heart of the experience of prayer.

4
Daniel 11: Patterns in History

A Question of Genre

In every culture there are literary 'genres.' The form and style in which something is written tends to be related to the nature of the contents and the purpose for which it is written. Failure to recognize the genre of what you are reading can lead to misunderstanding what it says. This is particularly likely to happen when reading something from a different culture, because you may be unaware of its genres, or misunderstand them because they seem like ones you know when they are not.

The long, enigmatically phrased, survey of history in Daniel 11 has no analogy elsewhere in the Hebrew Bible. In 1964 Grayson and Lambert published some texts which they called 'Akkadian Prophecies' and drew attention to similarities between them and Daniel 8.23–25 and 11.3–45.[20] Some of these texts had been published before, and a possible link with Daniel noted. This fresh publication, bringing together previously known material and adding new material, stimulated new interest in these texts. This led to the uncovering of new texts belonging to this group and of new copies or further fragments of the known texts. There are now five 'core' texts: The Marduk Prophecy; the Shulgi Prophecy; the Dynastic Prophecy; the Uruk Prophecy; and Text A. At least two other texts, Text B and LBAT 1543, have similarity to this group.

The Marduk and Shulgi Prophecies have introductions presenting them as speeches by the god Marduk and king Shulgi (king of Ur *ca* 2094–2047 BCE) respectively. Whatever introduction the other three 'core' texts have is broken off or too damaged to make sense. All five texts are purported prophecies that take the form of concise surveys of a series of rulers' reigns. The rulers are unnamed, but referred to as 'a king/prince' or as 'king of X.' In most cases plausible correlations can be made between the rulers and events alluded to in the texts and known historical rulers and events. If the texts originate from not long after the latest event they record, they come from various dates between the 12th century (The Marduk Prophecy) and the 3rd century (The Dynastic Prophecy) BCE. The following short extract from the Uruk Prophecy is typical of their form and content.[21]

---

20   A K Grayson and W G Lambert, 'Akkadian Prophecies' *Journal of Cuneiform Studies* 18 (1964) pp 7–30. Akkadian is the language of which ancient Assyrian and Babylonian were dialects.

21   H Hunger and S A Kaufmann, 'A new Akkadian Prophecy Text' *Journal of the American Oriental Society* 95 (1975) pp 371–375. The lines quoted are from the reverse of the clay tablet.

9.   After him a king will arise, but he as well will not provide justice for the land, he will not give the right decisions for the land.

10. He will subdue the world, and all the world will tremble at the mention of his name.

11. But after him a king will arise in Uruk who will provide justice in the land and will give right decisions for the land.

12. He will establish the right of the cult of Anu in Uruk.

13. He will remove the protective goddess of Uruk from Babylon and let her dwell in her own sanctuary in Uruk.

14. The people belonging to her he will devote to her. He will rebuild the temple of Uruk and restore the sanctuaries of the gods.

15. He will renew Uruk. The gates of Uruk he will build of lapis lazuli. He will fill the rivers and fields with abundant yield.

16. After him his son will arise as king in Uruk and become master of the world.

17. He will exercise rule and kingship in Uruk and his dynasty will be established forever.

18. The kings of Uruk will exercise rulership like the gods.

There are significant points of similarity between Daniel 11 and these prophecies.[22] They report historical events in a concise, annalistic style with people referred to enigmatically and the verbs in the future tense. The Akkadian Prophecies use the phrase '(after him) a king shall arise' as a 'section divider.' Daniel 11 has no regular 'section divider' but does use two similar phrases a number of times ('X shall arise' in vv 2, 3, 7; 12.1; 'after him shall arise' in vv 20, 21). These phrases do not occur in the Hebrew Bible outside of Daniel. Another similarity between Daniel and the Akkadian Prophecies is the command to seal up the book in Daniel 12.4. The Dynastic Prophecy ends with a 'secrecy colophon': 'A secret of the great gods. You may show it to the initiated, but to the uninitiated you must not show it.'

The stylistic and verbal similarities make it plausible to suggest a link between the Akkadian Prophecies and Daniel 8.23–25 and 11.2–12.4. This is made all the more likely by the fact that no comparable material is known from elsewhere, including Egypt and Greece, antedating Daniel. Another consideration is that the language of the Akkadian Prophecies is closely related to the specialized vocabulary and writing system used in Mesopotamian omens, and we have seen probable links with this omen literature in the imagery of Daniel 7 and 8. All this fits with the visions of Daniel coming from someone who is well versed in 'the literature and language of the Chaldeans' (Daniel 1.4).

---

22   For a more detailed discussion see Lucas, 'Daniel: Resolving the Enigma,' pp 73–76.

What might be the implications for our understanding of the passages in Daniel if they are consciously modelled on the genre of the Akkadian Prophecies? What does it suggest about their nature and purpose? The Akkadian Prophecies seem to have been written after most of the events they describe. They are probably constructed from existing records such as the 'Chronicles' (records of major events in a king's reign) and 'historical omens' (omens related to actual past historical events). Therefore their purpose was not to *predict* the course of history but to *interpret* it. In particular, the purpose was to explain the current situation, and sometimes to legitimate it.[23] In some cases the closing lines seem to look to the immediate future (such as lines 16–18 in the Uruk Prophecy above). This suggests that the importance of the passages in Daniel is not whether or not they are predictions of events, but in the interpretation they give of history. Of particular importance will be how the earlier history bears on the situation dealt with at the end of the survey of history, and what might flow from it.

Patterns in History

In Daniel 11.2–12.4 there is a handful of Hebrew verbal roots which occur with particular frequency. English translations tend to use more than one word to translate each root: 'arise/stand/raise' (used 16 times); 'come/attack/bring' (used 12 times); 'turn/return/do again' (used 12 times); 'make/ act/do' (used 10 times). Repetition of these roots contributes to the drawing of patterns in the history recounted. Kings rise to power and achieve a measure of success by attacking others. This often provokes attacks in retaliation. Conflict ebbs and flows. Some kings achieve considerable power, but then fall unexpectedly.

The careers of four particular kings stand out: the 'warrior king' of vv 3–4, the 'king of the north' of vv 10–19, the king of v 20 and the 'contemptible person' of vv 21–45.[24] The amount of space given to the last figure indicates that he is the focus of the survey. Some aspects of his career are foreshadowed by those of the earlier kings. Like the warrior king and previous king of the north he is able to 'do as he pleases' (vv 3b, 16, 36a). Like the king of the north he invades 'the beautiful land' (vv 16, 41) and gains some support there (vv 14, 30b, 32a). Both make treacherous agreements (vv 17, 23) and meet a check during their rise to power (vv 18b, 30a). The king of the north shows a hint of the hubris of the contemptible person (vv 12a, 36a, 37b). Like the king of v 20, the contemptible person is concerned with exacting tribute and amassing wealth (vv 28, 43).

23 M Jong Ellis, 'Observations on Mesopotamian Oracles and Prophetic Texts' *Journal of Cuneiform Studies* 41 (1989) pp 127–186, especially pp 171–186.

24 These are generally understood to be Alexander the Great, Antiochus III (the Great), Seleucus IV and Antiochus IV (Epiphanes).

The fact that the careers of the earlier kings foreshadow that of the contemptible person prepares the reader for the fact that, despite his much greater success, his career, like theirs, will come to an untimely end (vv 4a, 19, 20b). In fact, throughout the account of his career there are reminders that there is a limit set to it (vv 24b, 35, 36b, 40a) before it is reached (v 45b). There can be no doubt that the point of this 'patterning' is to assure those who are suffering under Antiochus Epiphanes that his rule is limited and will meet an untimely end. The description of that end in vv 40–45 does not describe how the end actually came about. These verses are best seen not as a detailed prediction of it, but as a confident assertion that it must come, expressed using words borrowed from earlier prophets, especially from Isaiah's prophecies about the downfall of Assyria because of her hubris—another example of the re-application of Scripture.[25]

There is a similar 'patterning' of history in Daniel 8. The mention of Belshazzar in v 1 does not only provide a dating. It invites a comparison between the content of the story in chapter 5 and this vision. To some extent Belshazzar is a pale foreshadowing of the little horn. He desecrated the vessels from the Temple (8.11–12) and his fate was sealed by a hand sent from heaven (8.25c). The repetition of words and phrases creates a clear pattern in the careers of the ram, the goat and the little horn.[26] The ram 'became great' (v 4c), the goat 'grew exceedingly great' (v 8a) and the little horn 'grew exceedingly great…It grew as high as the host of heaven' (vv 9a, 10a). The 'power' of each is stressed (vv 4b, 7b–8, 24). The end of each is expressed in terms of a being 'broken' (vv 7a, 8b, 25c). The ram's horns are broken by the goat, but no agent is expressed with regard to the breaking of the goat's horn (no doubt implying an act of God), and it is explicitly stated that the breaking of the little horn is not the work of a human agent. In the latter two cases the references are to Alexander's sudden death by fever and Antiochus' sudden death, due to an unspecified illness. Once again it seems clear that the purpose of this 'patterning' is to assure those who are suffering at Antiochus' hand that although he seems to tower over the land and be invincible, his power will collapse.

Judgment in History

The patterns that are drawn in Daniel 8 and 11 are not simply imposed on history—they are recognized in it and drawn out of it. There is a similarity here with the work of the teachers of 'wisdom' in ancient Israel. They looked for such patterns at various levels of experience and expressed them in proverbs. One pattern they found was, 'Pride goes before destruction,

---

25 On Daniel's re-use of earlier prophetic oracles see: M Fishbane, *Biblical Interpretation*, pp 489–495.
26 These are generally taken to be Darius III, Alexander the Great and Antiochus IV (Epiphanes).

and a haughty spirit before a fall' (Proverbs 16.18). The author of Daniel sees this pattern writ large on the stage of international politics. The arrogance that may come with success and power can lead rulers and nations to over-reach themselves in various ways that contribute to their downfall. It can also provoke envy and opposition and a grasping for power from both within and without, which leads to collapse. H Butterfield, then Professor of Modern History in the University of Cambridge, wrote an essay on 'Judgment in History' in 1949:

> There seems to be one fundamental law of a very solemn kind which touches this question of judgment; and when I turn to the ancient prophets and recall the limited area of history they had at their disposal for making inductions, I am always surprised at the curious aptness with which they seem to have found the formula in this connection—a formula which they put in a special position of priority. Judgment in history falls heaviest on those who come to think of themselves as gods, who fly in the face of Providence and history, who put their trust in man-made systems and worship the work of their own hands, who say that the strength of their own right arm gave them the victory.[27]

Butterfield wrote from an avowedly Christian perspective. But what he said is supported by a recent purely secular analysis of 'judgment in history' (though the author does not use that phrase) by Prof Paul Kennedy.[28] Walter Brueggemann comments that

> Kennedy's book is a cold, social scientific analysis, and Kennedy apparently would resist any move to introduce a moral dimension into his calculus. It occurs to me, however, that Kennedy's analysis, given in very different categories, is not far removed from the prophetic analysis. It is the characteristic urging of Israel's prophets that arrogant nations, which overreach in imagined self-sufficiency, operate autonomously at their own peril.[29]

These patterns, which the Hebrew sages and prophets discerned, are not like physical laws. They do not operate in an inexorable, predictable way—but they are there. They arise from factors inherent in human nature and the world as created by God. Even when there is no clear evidence of God at work opposing evil, the presence of this particular pattern of judgment in

27 H Butterfield, *Christianity and History* (London: Fontana, 1964) p 82.
28 P Kennedy, *The Rise and Fall of the Great Powers* (London: Fontana, 1989).
29 W Brueggemann, *Theology of the Old Testament* (Minneapolis: Fortress Press, 1997) p 526.

history, which Daniel exposes, gives some hope that history is not totally out of control morally. Recognition of it would give some comfort to those experiencing the arrogant defiance of their God by Antiochus Epiphanes.

Daniel's Patterns and the Preacher

Daniel does not sit very easily in a postmodern environment. Postmodern people, we are told, are averse to metanarratives and Daniel's 'patterns in history' are a form of metanarrative—an over-arching story which integrates and interprets the smaller narratives within history.

People seem to be averse to metanarratives for at least two reasons. One is the claim that they are not real, but are simply imposed on history by those who look for them. Both Butterfield and Kennedy, looking at history from very different perspectives, are witnesses against this view as far as Daniel's patterns are concerned. The other reason is the claim that metanarratives are 'oppressive.' They are used by those who invent them to impose their views and ways of doing things on other people. This does not fit Daniel's use of patterns. His is a view from the 'under-side.' At the heart of Daniel 8 is the question, 'How long?' (v 13) voiced by those who are oppressed by someone who is forcing *his* metanarrative on Jews. Antiochus took to himself the title 'epiphanes' because he saw himself as 'god manifest,' an incarnation of the deity. Daniel empowers the oppressed by challenging this metanarrative with another one, one that is rooted in human experience and history.

The challenge for preachers is to expose current false metanarratives and their oppressive effects. However, instead of dismissing all metanarratives, they must then catch the hearers' imagination with an alternative, real, liberating Christian metanarrative.